MOTHER LODE

Montana
Poems and Narratives

by Joe Beardsley

S0-BVV-449

Tobacco Root Mountains Press

MOTHER LODE

Montana
Poems and Narratives

by Joe Beardsley

To Norma —

Best Wishes —

Joe
Beardsley

Front Cover Photos:
 −Looking Across Virginia City up Alder Gulch, by Jerry Brekke
 −Virginia City Main Street, adapted from a historic photo of
   Virginia City, Montana

Back Cover Photo by Leita Beardsley
Cover Design by Lisa Beardsley, Leita Beardsley, Michael Dougherty
Cover Production by Michael Dougherty

Publishing Consultant: Michael Dougherty

Jo The Clown first appeared in the Spring-Summer, 1990 Issue of Rocky
Mountain Poetry Magazine

First Edition

Copyright © 1997 by Joe Beardsley
Published by Tobacco Root Mountains Press

ALL RIGHTS RESERVED. NO PART OF THIS BOOK MAY BE REPRODUCED
IN ANY FORM OR BY ANY ELECTRONIC OR MECHANICAL MEANS
INCLUDING INFORMATION STORAGE AND RETRIEVAL SYSTEMS
WITHOUT PERMISSION IN WRITING FROM THE PUBLISHER, EXCEPT BY A
REVIEWER WHO MAY QUOTE BRIEF PASSAGES IN A REVIEW.

ISBN: 0-9654056-0-5
Library of Congress Catalog Card Number: 96-90781

For Information or More Copies of Mother Lode, Contact:

Tobacco Root Mountains Press
100 Jewett Lane
Three Forks, MT   59752
(406) 285-3119

PRINTED IN THE UNITED STATES OF AMERICA

—For—

All of the family

In Memory Of
  My Mother
  and Father
  and the Friends who were here, and walked
  these hills,
  and knew so well these meadows of the heart

*Life is short
        but the days are long*

A Portion of the Proceeds
FromThe Sale of This Book
Will be Donated Toward
The Preservation of
Historic

VIRGINIA CITY, MONTANA

Contents

Acknowledgments

Daughter Lisa, whose honest support has always been an encouragement for me in the sometimes discouraging activity of writing anything, and whose natural art and trips with me to shoot pictures and search through archives has contributed so greatly to the selection of photos included in this book

Wife Leita, who, in spite of it's eons-long birth, has supported this piece of work, and whose perceptive judgement has always served to make it better

Gwen Petersen, who not only loves writing and publishing, but who encourages others to do so, and without whose motivation techniques this book might have waited publication another twenty years

The Livingston Writer's Group for their patient listening and thoughtful critiques

Jerry Brekke and Jim Derleth for a great summer day spent prowling the hills above Virginia City

Everyone, from far and near, who so enthusiastically dug up and provided to me photos for use in this book

Dick Dillof for his encouraging words, and fireside sing-alongs

Preface

I grew up in Virginia City, Montana, experiencing the deep, drifting, long-lasting snows of winter (winters were *much* worse in those days), the rich-silted, rushing waters of Alder Gulch, the soft muds of spring, and the peaceful summers of a small, beginning tourist town.

There in Virginia City my first life awareness seemed to be of the hard times associated with World War II and the joy when the "boys" came home.

I never really saw my town until I had grown, started a family, and been gone away for a long time. Then, one day I came home to visit, and there it was, nestled among the hills, against the higher backdrop of timbered ridges. I finally understood why so many tourists raved and fell in love with the place, and I suddenly gained an understanding of my own homesickness.

The memories, faces, sounds, smells, feelings run deep for me, and root me to Virginia City in such a way that none of it can be separated from what I am—one of her native sons.

I am older now, and have come to see that this peculiar, shaping bond ties me not only to Virginia City, but to Montana, and to the West, and to America.

The writings in this book were born from the homesickness, the deeply grained memories of the folks, the pain and joy of a harder, different time, the good, green hills of my boyhood home.

J.J.B.

Pointing Them North

In the 1880's, a young cowboy named Teddy "Blue" Abbott drove cattle from Texas to Montana. In the 1930's, Helen Huntington Smith interviewed Teddy Blue who was by then an old man, and wrote his story.

We Pointed Them North is a story told by a genuine cowboy, about a kind of people and a kind of country that have largely passed from our experience.

The song, "Pointing Them North" was not just inspired by Teddy Blue; it is about Texas, and Montana, and all the good land and people in between.

Pointing Them North

It's a long ride from Texas to Montana's sweet meadows
    he's traveled it a number of times,
Mixin' up dreams of good whiskey and women
    with songs that just ran through his mind.
To the sound of the night bird he sang to the night herd
    days and nights melted away,
Just like the memories of an old Texas cowboy
    who's livin' one more yesterday.

White-painted walls in a home for the aged
    are not what he sees in his mind,
He rides through the days in a rockin' chair saddle
    crossin' the rivers of time.
His white hair is black now, the sun's on his back now
    the Stetson's pulled low on his eyes,
He still feels the chaps, the boots and six-shooter,
    and a spirit that never did die.

And he's pointing them north once again
To the beautiful places he's been
Let sun, wind and weather come whip him to leather
His life is about to begin
He's pointing them north once again.

The afternoon sun's layin' warm through the window
    his old white head nods for awhile,
He's seein' the face—a young Shoshone woman—
    he remembers the tease in her smile.
He's dreamin' the years, and the laughter and tears
    they shared as a man and a wife,

Livin' in love in the little log cabin
    and the good ways she warmed up his life.

The sun is now leavin' long shadows of evenin'
    his head is bowed low and is still,
In comes a young nurse, sweet-smilin' and sayin'
    Time now for your afternoon pill.
She'll gently shake him, tryin' to wake him
    to his world of livin' alone,
Where he always believed in the day he would leave
    on his long awaited ride home.

And he's pointing them north once again . . .

Horse Shoe Bar beef herd on the way to the railroad,
Badlands of the Missouri River, September 2, 1896
—*Photo courtesy The Montana Historical Society, Helena*

Silver Buckles

Montana has always produced its share of rodeo cowboys, most of them remaining local, developing a local following, acquiring a local fame. A handful have gone on to bigger prizes, and a few have actually ridden into the rarified air at the top.

One summer morning a local newspaper carried the picture of a former rodeo king working alone on his tractor in the middle of a hayfield. That image slowly gathered itself in my mind.

"Silver Buckles" is a song about memories. It belongs to everyone who ever tried, to everyone who ever succeeded, to everyone who ever dreamed.

Silver Buckles

I rose up with the mornin' sun,
Knowin' it had just begun
Warmin' the fields of meadow hay;
I felt the feelin' risin',
And it wasn't too surprisin'
My mind was goin' back to a better day.
I drove the tractor till midmornin'
When it quit without a warnin',
So I walked away and left it in the field;
The bunkhouse yard is shady,
And as fragrant as a lady
With a sweet perfume and feminine appeal.

I can see beyond the mornin'
Where mountain clouds are formin'
Big thunderheads that billow in the blue;
Within those ivory castles
My mind don't have the hassles
Of the daily chores I just don't want to do.
My mind goes back a'dreamin'
Till I see the banners streamin'
And I touch those big arenas one more time,
Where I rode in all the biggest shows,
The silver-studded rodeos,
Tryin' to make those silver buckles mine.

Silver buckles, silver buckles
Are the mark of a champion;
Silver buckles,
How bright those silver buckles
That I finally won.

I won the silver buckles,
Such trustin' to your luck'll
Either make it big or really let you down;
The money I was makin'
Wasn't easy for the takin',
I dearly paid my way from town to town.
I rode the brahmas and the barebacks,
And the talent that I might have lacked
I made up for in luck and hangin' on;
I know that was my better day,
I know I've got to mow the hay,
I know my silver buckle days are gone.

But within my deepest dreamin'
I still hear the people screamin',
They came to see me ride, they knew my name;
'Round the chutes they told the story
How I rode my way to glory
Ridin' bulls and broncs into the halls of fame

World All-Around Champion, Hall-of-Fame Cowboy Benny Reynolds,
Twin Bridges, Montana, aboard Moose Milk—San Angelo, 1967
—*Photo courtesy Ferrell Butler, Red Oak, Texas*

Oley

Virginia City, Montana was born through the white man's search for gold. That history can still be seen marking the surrounding countryside—the hand diggins', the creeks and gulches torn by monster dredges, the shacks, shafts and tunnels of the hardrock miner.

In my earliest days there, some of those old miners and prospectors who had carved the marks remained, sitting outside on the streets in the sun of the short summers, or inside warm barrooms during the long winters. To me, they seemed like relics of better days—haunted by memories of dreams that had broken, worn to nothing by lives that had failed.

I wrote the song, "Oley", based on an incident that happened to one of those old miners back in the late '40's when I was a boy.

Oley

His last claim was a bar stool
 in the Blasting-Cap Saloon
Where he drank away the pension
 that he'd earned;
His memories ran to summer nights
 and howlin' at the moon
In the days before the lessons
 that he learned.

His cough was still a token
 of the mines, his hands were broken
Like pieces of the hardrock
 that he'd drilled;
And when the day was shuttered,
 he took his ghosts and muttered
To them, all the way to his cabin
 on the hill.

His mind would often hunger
 for the times when he was younger
When he loved to share
 the good light of day
With the honey-haired woman
 who waited in the cabin,
Till the cold winter
 took her away.

He made no excuses
 for the breaks and the bruises,
The pain that a man
 must go through;

The dreams he created
    were a long time outdated—
He was a man
    who never came true.

Oh, what were you Oley,
    in the days of your youth
When you thought you held the world
    in your strong young hands?
The hardrock mines
    finally taught you the truth:
The world is much bigger
    than a man.

One night he left the barroom
    in the middle of December,
He didn't feel
    the forty-two below;
He walked into the springtime
    with a girl that he remembered,
He crossed the bridge
    and lay down in the snow.

She came to him through a rainbow,
    she lay down by his side,
She held him and her kisses
    lit the dreams
Of a long ago love
    that had never ever died;
Oley, do you hear
    the angels sing?

This Virginia City cabin still sits across the road, northwest
of the old Brewery, not far from where Oley's cabin stood
— *Photo by the author*

Mother Lode

Gold found in a mountain creek— "easier" gold— is panned, sluiced and dredged by placer miners. But theory holds that the creek gold was gouged by a glacier or eroded through some other natural force out into daylight from deep in the innermost, secret, hardrock heart of the earth. There lies a far greater treasure, not easy for the takin' like the chickenfeed found in the creek, but hidden, waiting to be discovered by that special, persistent, committed to a life of hardship miner who will settle for nothing less than the one great prize of all prizes, the Mother Lode.

The mountains around Virginia City have felt the trudging boots of the lode seeker. As a young man just out of high school, I worked for one of these men. I helped drive a long tunnel deep into the bowels of Baldy mountain, eight miles south of town. We found nothing.

The song, "Mother Lode", is dedicated to those driven seekers who can not settle for anything less than the ultimate reward. Often, the reward is not what the seeker expects.

Mother Lode

You see I am an old man
    sittin' in the morning sun
On a wooden bench
    outside the General Store.
This has been a gold rush town,
    but the days of gold are done,
Now tourists bring 'new gold'
    up to the door.

Why don't you come and sit with me?
    I've noticed you today
And I peg you as the kind
    who'd like to know
A bit of my family history,
    we go back quite a way,
We came to the Ruby Valley
    years ago.

Some raised hay in mountain meadows,
Some drove cattle by the river,
Some brought pans and shovels
And dug for the gravel gold;
But I had a different dream,
It lay on the mountain ridges
Where I tramped ten-thousand miles
    in my search
For the Mother Lode.

I remember my old Grandad,
    how he always was a gambler,
On a cut of cards or cattle

he would lay his money down;
My Daddy was no different,
    with the spirit of a rambler,
And neither was a stranger to
    the hardrock underground.

I fell heir to mountains,
    to dreams of golden fountains
That once had run in rivers into
    molten pools of gold,
More elusive than a rainbow,
    more alluring than a woman,
She burned me in her summer heat,
    she froze me in her cold.

I roomed with bats and mountain cats,
    it almost seemed they knew me,
I weathered every broken heart
    that came down through the years,
I learned how much a man can need
    the warm arms of a woman,
I cried out to the mountains, but
    they never seemed to hear.

And then one day I found it—
    It had rainbows all around it—
It glistened in my carbide lamp,
    I knew my search was done;
But the glory stole my senses,
    and I wandered in the mountains—
Folks later said I'd crossed a ridge
    and gazed upon the sun . . .

Our children all are grown and gone
  away into the city,
I think each one is searchin' for
  some kind of a Mother Lode,
But trouble is a way of life,
  and doesn't have much pity
For those who set their foot upon
  some kind of a wanderin' road;

But searchin' has it's own rewards
  quite apart from findin',
If you can stand the heartache
  of a long and lonely road;
Now if you think you'd care to try
  you won't need no remindin',
If you've got five bucks, I've got a map
  that'll lead you to the Mother Lode

Boats

It is early spring. The rain has stopped and the streets
lay pooled in water and mud. The morning smells wet and the
sky remains overcast, filtering gray light through to the small,
silent town. Birds sing bright songs seeming to contrast the
dismal day.

The small boy moves slowly in the mud along the roiling
creek. Too young for school, too old to stay inside, he gives no
thought to the consequences of his work, to the mud streaked
up and over the tops of his red rubber pull-on boots, to the
soggy blue pants or the streaked red jacket. It is war time in the
world, and in the town he has felt the mood of it.

The creek, chocolate with mountain snow water, leaps
and tumbles and sings past him; it adds its smell of mud and
damp to the wet day. A short distance from the creek the alder
bush springs from the moist earth, extending tender, leafed
shoots to the sky. The boy slogs from the creek to the bush
where he chatters and sings to himself as he gathers leaves into
his tiny hands. Then he returns, kneels beside the water, and
carefully launches the leaves into the current. They circle close
to the bank, drifting slowly down, eddying, then one by one
they are caught and whisked away on the strong current.

They are boats. They contain soldiers with boots and uniforms
and helmets and guns. They are going away, and he feels for
them the feelings he has picked up from the mood of the town.
A fear and a sadness. A longing and a loneliness. And a courage.

Good-bye, he calls and he waves. He feels it pulling him,
aching in his stomach and heart. Hand motionless in the air
now, he watches till the boats are gone.

Alder Creek, just south of Virginia City, clear and cold in April,
waiting for the first melting mountain snows of spring
—Photo by the author

Hardrock Miner

*As a young man I worked underground in Alder Gulch, Montana
and in the lead/zinc Mayflower Mine in the mountains northwest
of Heber, Utah. In both places I grew in the skills of mucking,
timbering, cussing, and running a jackleg drill.*

*The jackleg drill is an air driven jackhammer-like drill mounted
atop a telescoping steel leg which is controlled by an air valve
located on the side of the drill.*

*Running a jackleg drill is an art based on sound, sight, feel and
balance. In hardrock miner terminology, it is known as a
'machine', and can push you, pull you, jerk and slam you, pinch
you, frustrate you (I once saw a man beat a jackleg with an ax), or
work so sweetly under your touch you take pride in running every
steel right "up to the chuck."*

*I liked the job as well as any I ever had, except for the fact I almost
got killed a couple of times, and the fact that everything in the mine
seemed to be heavier than I was, and I was supposed to pick it up
and work with it.*

*Several years ago, Merle Haggard had a hit song which paid tribute
to the truck driver.*

Well, this is my tribute to the hardrock miner.

Hardrock Miner

I'm a hardrock miner and I know how it feels
Headin' underground with a fist full of steel
I'm a hardrock miner breakin' rock for the mill
My muscles are as hard as the rock I drill

When I started in the mines I was down on my luck
Twelve years old when I learned how to muck
Since that time, wherever I roam
A hardrock tunnel has been my home.
As long as I'm strong, as long as I'm lean
I'll work underground with my drillin' machine
I'll break that rock till I break my back
'Cause my Daddy swung a nine-pound doublejack.

I'm a hardrock miner and I know how it feels
Headin' underground with a fist full of steel
I'm a hardrock miner and I earn my pay
Blastin' forty tons of rock down every day

When the boss said to me, "Can you run a machine?"
I said, "I'll turn more steel than you ever have seen;
I'll run your tunnel right through this hill
'Cause I make sweet music with a jackleg drill!"
Said the boss, "We ain't had no rock for days!"
So I took my drill and I climbed the raise;
I drilled 'er, and I loaded, and I gave 'er some room
And the whole mountain trembled
                    to my BOOM BOOM BOOM!

I'm a hardrock miner and I know how it feels
Headin' underground with a fist full of steel
I'm a hardrock miner workin' hard as I can
I understand the life of a hardrock minin' man.

After I've blasted the rock all down
I change my clothes and head for town
Where I swig rye whiskey 'till I've had my fill
And tell 'em how I run that jackleg drill.
I've got a pretty woman and her name is Lil
She asks me if I love her still
When it comes to women, I love you, Lil
But when I'm in the mine I love my jackleg drill!

One night I left the mine and went down town
To a place where them truck drivers hang around
As I walked through the door the place grew still
They were eyein' up a man who runs a jackleg drill;
They could see I was lean, they could see I was tough
They could see by my eye that I took no guff;
Finally Merle turned and said to Bill:
"Takes a special breed of man to run a jackleg drill!"

I'm a hardrock miner and I know how it feels
Headin' underground with a fist full of steel
I'm a hardrock miner working hard as I can
I'm mighty proud to be a hardrock minin' man!

Hardrock miner running a jackleg drill

—*Photo courtesy Jim VanGundy—Spokane, WA/Hecla Mining*

Rudy M. Broksle, the author's stepfather, hardrock miner, ready
to go underground, Anselmo Mine, Butte, Montana — 1937
—Photo courtesy Rudy M. Broksle

Rudy M. Broksle, hardrock miner, rancher, artist, world traveler
Anselmo Mine, Butte, Montana — 1996
—*Photo by the author*

Mountain Man

The saga of the mountain man holds a myth and mystique that have only increased with time.

Man brings changes upon himself through his own thirst for freedom, excitement and adventure.

Many of us do not like the changes we are seeing in Montana and the west right now. I'm sure the mountain men disliked the changes they saw toward the end of their time. Maybe it is a good thing that each generation only briefly inherits the earth.

Mountain Man

From windblown ridges to broadwater valleys
I've taken the heat and the cold
And never forgotten the songs of the Mountains
What they did to my heart
 and my soul

Mountain Man
Carryin' my rifle and my life in my hands
One horse to saddle, another to pack
Big sky above me, sun on my back
If you see me I won't be the same
I don't care if you never know my name
Places I'm goin', things that I see
Give me the reasons I have to be
 a Mountain Man

I came to the mountains, left cities far away
Left it all behind me and found a better way
Wearin' my leather in the winter and the fall
Sometimes in the summer wearin'
 nothin' at all

I've fought the Native, yet I know he's my friend
We're both grievin' for the message I send
Back to the cities sayin', "Follow! Come along!"
When they follow, he and I
 will be gone

From windblown ridges to broadwater valleys
I've taken the heat and the cold
And never forgotten the songs of the Mountains
What they did to my heart
          and my soul

   Mountain Man!

       Mountain Man!

             M
              O
                U
                  N
                    T
                      A
                        I
                      N
                        MAN !

Joseph L. Meek—Mountain Man

—Photo courtesy The Montana Historical Society, Helena

Headin' Home To Butte, Montana

I grew up in Virginia City, Montana. My experience touched mainly small towns and the solitude of mountains. The big city in my life was Butte, Montana.

In those days, Butte, driven by its robust underground mining economy, thronged with a melting pot of people—Irish, Finns, Serbs, Swedes, Norwegians, English, Dutch, Greek, Italians. They created the character of Butte out of their own characters—tough, fighting, undiscouraged, 'give you the shirt' hearts of gold.

I've always loved the raucous, poignant history of Butte. I wrote the song, "Headin' Home To Butte, Montana", thinking of a time when the underground mines were still in full swing.

Headin' Home To Butte, Montana

Headin' home to Butte, Montana,
Got a cowboy hat and a red bandanna,
    Levi jacket, boots, and faded jeans.
I made no money in the rodeo,
But I learned things I didn't know,
    and grew a little older so it seems.

Had a chance to have my pockets full
'Till I lost pull on a Brahma bull,
    now all I've got is someone on my mind.
When I get back to Butte, Montana,
One thing that I understand is
    I still have a friend that I can find.

And you're a hard livin', hard driven',
Hard rockin', tough talkin' town;
You've got a hold on me, like an old friend of mine;
I call you home, and when I settle down,
I'll give my love to your loveliest lady
And my body to your hardrock mines.

Headin' home to Butte, Montana,
With a teardrop on my red bandanna,
    but a smile just turned the corners of my mind.
Starlight brings it to my eyes,
Scenes I'm glad to recognize,
    and memories I thought I'd left behind.

About a mile farther on,
I'll see them in the early dawn,
    your gleamin' lights across the Harding Way.

Tears of joy, a shout, a song,
Lord my feelin's are runnin' strong,
    and I'm just glad I'm comin' home today.

Though I'll always want to be a rodeo cowboy,
    I'll be whatever I can;
Right now all I really want to be
    is in the arms of Mary Ann.
Sometimes I'm just takin' my time
    old town, are you really my friend?
Many good men have gone down in your mines
    and never seen daylight again.

Gallows Frame against a summer sky, Anselmo Mine,
Butte, Montana — 1996

—Photo by the author

Hardrock Miner drilling with a drifter mounted on a single-screw
column underground somewhere in Montana—probably early 1930's
—*Photo courtesy The Montana Historical Society, Helena*

Mary McGovern in the doorway of Hannah and Mary's Store,
Virginia City Montana — 1930's
—Photo courtesy The Montana Historical Society, Helena

BIRDSEYE VIEW of VIRGINIA CITY, MONTANA FROM "BUMMER DAN BAR."

View of Virginia City from Bummer Dan's Bar, west of town, streets
unpaved, before the dredges came — exact date unknown
—Photo courtesy The Montana Historical Society, Helena

Les Stiles, cowboy, stagecoach driver, and Dick Pace, author, journalist, hoisting one in Bob's Place, Virginia City — 1986
—*Photo Dick Pace collection, courtesy Thompson~Hickman County Library*

The Parker Homestead, smallest State Park in Montana,
Highway 287, seven miles southwest of Three Forks

—Photo by the author

Josephine Jewett samples her own cider after a day of pressing apples
on her place at Granite Creek, north of Virginia City — 1983
—*Photo by Sheila Beardsley*

The Lady, The Drifter,
And The Summer Breeze

The heart of the wanderer beats to some degree within all of us. It manifests itself on that first truly warm day with the touch of that first soft breeze and the sight of an open road leading anywhere. Most of us smile, tip our hat to the muse, close a glass door on it, and go quietly back to our ordinary lives.

Others answered the call. They came west to the Rockies, on foot, on horseback, in wagons, in Model T's, on the rails.

We see their descendants today, trudging beside a ribbon of oil, following the sun with backpack and raised thumb. These are the restless ones, whose eyes continually search the clouds beyond the farthest ridge, whose faces mirror the image of mountain, river, prairie—the lonely country.

But freedom, in all its glory, never comes without a price.

The Lady, The Drifter,
And The Summer Breeze

I kissed her in the springtime
    she was tender as a lily,
She thought that it was ring time,
    how could she be so silly?
She did not understand the way
    the summer breezes blow,
Driftin' to the Rockies from
    the Gulf of Mexico.

I said You know I love you
    but I'm followin' a summer breeze,
I'll be back to see you
    when the snow is on the ground,
I've saddled up a rainbow
    and I'm headin' for Montana,
Like a bird that learned to fly,
    I'm never comin' down;

If you want to love me
    you'll have to love a drifter,
A summer-season tumbleweed,
    a little bit of cloud,
A bluebird flyin' in the spring,
    a misty mornin' river,
The other side of mountains,
    and a field that isn't plowed.

The next time I saw her
    she had five thousand acres,
She was bein' courted by

the lawyers and the bakers,
She said she only loved one man,
    he's like the winds that blow,
Driftin' to the Rockies from
    the Gulf of Mexico.

I thought how much I loved her,
    I thought about the summer breeze,
I thought how cold the winter wind,
    the snow upon the ground,
Then I saw the clouds and lightnin'
    rollin' on the mountain,
Like a bird that learned to fly,
    I'm never comin' down;

If you want to love me
    you'll have to love a drifter,
A summer-season tumbleweed,
    a little bit of cloud,
A bluebird flyin' in the spring,
    a misty mornin' river,
The other side of mountains,
    and a field that isn't plowed.

How long will a man love loneliness,
How long will a man love pain,
How long will a man walk alone
In the cold, drivin' rain?
Until he learns the lessons
Of love soft and warm,
And then he cannot live without
A woman's lovin' arms.

I came back in early June,
    for waitin' I would thank her,
She said Hello, goodbye again,
    I'm married to a banker.
She said she knew she'd never tame
    the summer winds that blow,
Driftin' to the Rockies from
    the gulf of Mexico.

Bum Lambs And Beaver Dams

Life in the mountains has never been easy. Long, unrelenting winters, summers ridden with drought, late, muddy springs, falls that last for seven days before returning you to another long, unrelenting winter. The man of the mountains knows these things and finds beyond the harshness the true connected beauty that will always hold him there.

He loves the soft, deep snow falling silently into timber, the perfumes of springtime mountain meadows, the smell of pine in fall air, the abounding perpetuation of life, from the new to the old and again to the new. These permeate his breath and his blood, and his heart forever beats to them.

Ah, but there is the loneliness.

Bum Lambs And Beaver Dams

Hello to you, Miss Jenny Lou,
I had to see you today
And I see surprise right in your eyes
At me comin' here this way
I seldom roam from my mountain home
But I've left it far behind
'Cause you gave me the memory
Of love that I need to find.

You understand I'm just a mountain man,
I've got no fancy way
But I lately find that I fill my mind
With words that I need to say
About love, and yes, about loneliness,
About longin' day and night
My mind's on you Miss Jenny Lou,
Lord I hope this turns out right!

If you'd like bum lambs and beaver dams
And soft green mountain meadows
If you'd like the outside and trails to ride
And evenin' summer shadows
Winter nights with the northern lights
Like fire in the sky above
I need you Miss Jenny Lou
And I'll give you all my love.

Jenny I see it's time for me
To get down off the shelf
Starry nights are just not right
When you're sharin' 'em with yourself

And there comes a time in the lonesome pines
When lonesome just won't do
Jenny I see that a man like me
Needs a woman like you.

Orville Jewett, Leita's father, with traps and furs in front of the Parker
Homestead Cabin where the family lived in the early 1940's
—*Photo courtesy Josephine Jewett*

The Weather In Butte, Montana

Butte, Montana, with its mile-high mountain climate, provides weather experiences that sometimes border on the legendary. From sub-zero temperatures, to blizzards, bad roads and snowdrifts, and spring that never arrives—if that is what you want, they say, you will find it in Butte, Montana. But is it really true?

Here is the story of one fellow who went to Butte to find out for himself.

The Weather In Butte, Montana

They said Butte Montana was one cold hosanna
    from the first of July right through June
But I would not believe it, I could not receive it
    I did not make a judgement so soon.
By the first of September, how well I remember
    'twas fourteen good inches of snow
They said Don't be grinnin', the storm is beginnin'
    there's fourteen long months yet to go

It's forty below and I really don't know
How far down this crazy thermometer goes
I'm just wonderin' where it will end
I thought they were teasin'
When they said there's four seasons
June, July, August and Winter, my friend

By the first of the new year with the snow up to my ears
    and the temperature fallin' each day
They said Ain't it pretty, but you'd better get ready
    the big one is now on the way.
I said This is so fine, but show me the airline
    they said You won't fly out of here
The last plane that landed's been twenty months stranded
    just waitin' for the weather to clear

I said Can the jokes, now how come you nice folks
    all got stuck in a place like this?
They smiled and they said, with a shake of the head
    We don't know, we're just lucky we guess

Goin' Back

*Somewhere within each one of us lies a frontier, an unfenced,
unpaved, uninhabited place of solitude, a place for the broken spirit
to return and heal itself. For many, that place manifests itself in the
reality of the true American west, in the sound of its soil beneath
the feet, the feel of its its breezes across the face, the lure of its
unlimited places to roam free.*

*Also, for those who know that reality, has come the grief of change,
the paving over and locking up of good land by those who never
froze, never sweated, never watched their hopes bleed year by year
into the silent hills.*

*As the gritty, freedom-loving, hard-boned spirit of the west fades, so
also will fade the spirit of America and her children.*

Goin' Back

I

He's headin' out weary, battered and bruised
Tired of bein' treated like humanity refused
Goin' back to find himself again on the land
Pickin' up the pieces when he used to be a man
Leavin' the city for the Big Sky way
    ropin', ridin', and stackin' hay

Out on the highway he don't need a friend
He's laughin' at the miles, goin' back home again
Big smokin' diesel roll the hours behind
He's dreamin' of the good things he knows he will find
Sunshine and meadows, the place he was raised
    ropin', ridin', and stackin' hay

II

He waves to the driver and steps to the ground
Stops in amazement and stares all around
Big stores and blacktop are all that he sees
Where the old ranch-house and the good land used to be
Tears rollin' down his face he turns and walks away
Where cowboys don't ride the range anymore
    and farmers don't stack hay

He don't know where he's walkin', he's walkin all alone
Goin' back the way he came, but he can't find a home
Wonderin' why he has to see the things he has to see
Wonderin' why things have to be the way they have to be
Wonderin' why things never change, yet never stay the same
Where cowboys don't ride the range anymore
    and farmers don't stack hay

The Healing Place

Mutilated by an act of violence within a narrow window of time, she could never have become so scarred before the coming of the great machines or after the creation and enforcement of acute environmental protection laws. She had once sported a lively, alder-lined creek tumbling down between sagebrush hills; but when the machines came, they dammed her creek and floated themselves, and then gutted her, piling her rocks like bones to bleach in the sun.

No sooner was this violation finished than she began the slow, natural healing of herself. Most of her gold had been ripped away, but other good elements remained. The creek still flowed, but now, instead of leaping robustly between grassy, alder-lined banks, it wound slowly, eddied against the piles of rocks, drifted through and around them, forming serene pools and small ponds. In the spring, snow melted in the higher hills and mountains, and the creek swelled and gushed dark with mountain soil, and when it ebbed left much of that rich load silted among the rocks.

In the dry, late summer, wind lifted more soil from the hills and sprinkled it among the rocks, and in the early fall harvested seeds from the sage and tender grasses and sowed them into the new soil. Year after year, as the seasons worked their steady way with her, she slowly recovered from her deep wounds.

By the time the boy first discovered her, she had reclaimed such a soft shimmering beauty that he never noticed the old scars. He saw instead young pine trees strongly rooted, and quaking aspen with cedars mixed among them; he saw new alder clumps springing from the banks and islands, and fought his way through them, excited, fishing pole tangling; he saw cattails, and wide ponds and narrow ponds, and trails that wound over and around and among the piles of rocks, and, when he was older, carried his shotgun there on frosted

mornings where mallards would explode from sheltered coves almost beneath his feet, their quacks and whistling wings so stunning that he sometimes was almost unable to fire.

He crossed her multiple streams on beaver dams, and sometimes saw a beaver's little dog-nose gliding silently at the tip of a silken V, and when he made a motion there would be a whack and then nothing but circles on the water. He saw muskrats, tiny fur bodies hunched, intent on some strange muskrat work; he saw otter slides, and, in soft mud, tracks of deer. Eagles crossed on currents high above him, and he saw owls and knew they nested somewhere in the trees; sometimes hawks circled, hunting, spiraling up, their screams thrown down to him through the wind.

On soft summer days he loved to join her, sometimes with worm and spinner, sometimes with dry fly, soaked, muddied, hushed, expectant, enticing the trout; and sometimes, on hotter days, he exclaimed, disgusted, angry against the grey, laconic shapes who reposed in shaded water beneath overhanging willows, and ignored him.

Often he just lay in her grasses, dried and lulled by the sun, hearing a grasshopper clack, feeling the rush of a visiting dragon-fly, not even being remotely aware that, deep within him, she had begun the rich, fertile process of healing his own wounds. He dreamed in her warmth, and smelled her perfumes, mixed of the grass and the pines and cedars and the breeze and the cattails and the mud.

One afternoon a tourist traveled along the highway, noticing the scars of the old rape, the rocks hurled up to bleach in the sun. The tourist saw the soft, summer colors, felt the delicate, vibrant newness that now thrived here, sensed what the place really was, and what it could do. He drove slowly, letting the perfect air touch him through open car windows, briefly nursing his own regrets. Before moving on, before leaving the place forever behind, the tourist stopped and photographed a

thin boy trudging homeward in the golden evening,
mud-splattered, exhausted, and fiercely proud of the bounty
she'd yielded him: a green willow V bent with the weight of a
mess of fat trout.

Conrey Dredge #1 working near the mouth of Alder Gulch, piling up 'bones' to bleach in the sun — exact date unknown
—*Photo courtesy The Montana Historical Society, Helena*

Main Street of Virginia City in the sunshine on a winter day,
before the Bovey restoration had begun — exact date unknown
—*Photo courtesy The Montana Historical Society, Helena*

Virginia City oldtimer, Lou Romey, pannin' for color
somewhere in Alder Gulch, probably early 1940's
—*Photo Dick Pace collection, courtesy Thompson~Hickman County Library*

Charlie Bovey, the man who discovered and preserved the real Mother
Lode: an aging, original Virginia City, Montana — probably early 1940's
—Photo Dick Pace collection, courtesy Thompson~Hickman County Library

Wesley Williams sings to Elmarie Wendel at the Wells Fargo Coffeehouse
Cabaret, in 1952, the early days of the Virginia City Players
—*Photo Dick Pace collection, courtesy Thompson~Hickman County Library*

Sim Ferguson, oldtimer, takes sun on a winter day in front
of his Virginia City cabin — probably in the 1940's
—*Photo courtesy JoAn Garrison*

This Alder Gulch stone for Sim's wife still stands in the Virginia City
Hilltop Cemetery; Sim hauled, carved, and placed it himself
—*Photo Dick Pace collection, courtesy Thompson~Hickman County Library*

Cook and pie biter at work, somewhere on the
Montana open range — A. Huffman, photographer, 1886
—*Photo courtesy The Montana Historical Society, Helena*

Don Hanni shines Lou Romey's boots, as barber Harvey Romey looks
on; Don's dog, Laddie, waits — Virginia City, probably 1949
—*Photo Dick Pace collection, courtesy Thompson~Hickman County Library*

Cowboy Dreamin'

I have on several occasions lived in great cities of the American west. No matter which city, no matter which reason I lived there, the crush of that life always re-affirmed for me that my heart is rooted in Rocky Mountain solitude.

One morning, while living in one of those cities, I left the house to the clashing sound of traffic and the pungent, exhaust-laden taste of urban air. Memories of Montana flowed into my my mind.

By the time I'd driven fourteen blocks to work in a high-rise office building, "Cowboy Dreamin'" was ready to flow out of the tip of my pen.

Cowboy Dreamin'

It's a big city sunup and the traffic is hung up
For seven blocks outside my door
Takes a cup of black coffee to wake up my ulcers
And I know what I'd trade it all for:
A job as a cowboy in western Montana
Where I came from a long time before.

It's into the morning and another smog warning
As I face another day
I start up my engine, we both sit there coughin'
And then I am on my way
But I think of them cowboys in western Montana
(How much is a cowboy's pay?).

At my desk I'm wishin' I was fly fishin'
Up there on the Beaverhead
Where the phones are not ringin' and nobody's bringin'
Bad news the computers went dead
A cowboy's big worry in western Montana
Is keepin' them cattle fed.

It's someday I'm knowin' I will be goin'
Back there, and back there I'll stay
There will be no pity when I leave this city
Goin' back to the cowboy way
I'll even hunt coyotes in western Montana
(To hell with the EPA).

25 - 35 - 40 Below

Man never sees the real height of mountains to climb, the real depth of raging rivers to cross, or the real wind-chill of winters to survive. Whether this is a good thing, or a bad thing, doesn't really matter—for man is an easy dreamer.

25 - 35 - 40 Below

I headed west to the Rockies one day,
I said to my Darlin', "I'm goin' away;
There's cowboys, and gold, and grizzlies and all,
I'll make a big fortune, we'll marry next fall."

I met a tall stranger the very first day,
I said, "I'm needin' a job for some pay."
He laughed and he said, "Well, there's no jobs, you know,
When it's 25 - 35 - 40 below!"

We followed a gold rush as quick as we could,
Between just freezin' and choppin' up wood,
We never had time to go dig a small hole;
It was 25 - 35 - 40 below!

My friend said, "I'm tired of livin' this way,
I know how we both can go rustle some pay,
Robbin' stagecoaches and miners, you know,
When it's 25 - 35 - 40 below!"

Don't get me wrong now, don't misunderstand,
I always have been a most scrupulous man,
But you never know the way that a fellow will go,
When it's 25 - 35 - 40 below!

Our first job netted a sack of bad checks,
And some mad Vigilantes all wantin' our necks,
I said to my partner, "It's time that we go -
It's 25 - 35 - 40 below!"

He pulled out his pistol and aimed at my head,
He said, "I've a better ide'er instead -
You give me your boots and your coat, and then go;
It's 25 - 35 - 40 below!"

I limped home to my Darlin' one bright summer day,
She said, "Meet my husband, we were married in May
I couldn't be alone through that terrible cold -
It was 25 - 35 - would you believe - 40 below!"

April in Montana, and
Still too cold to dig for gold
—*Photo by Leita Beardsley*

Billy Apple's Crew

There are two basic ways to work underground as a hardrock miner: days pay, and contract.

The days pay man obviously receives a day's pay, which in my time was nineteen dollars and sixty cents, whether he breaks any rock or not. The contract miner, however, earns his pay based on the size of hole he has made. He is paid, as the poem says, for what he does. This pressure to produce causes the underground contract hardrock miner to become unusually skilled at his trade.

Billy Apple was the best contract miner I ever saw, and it was my privilege to work with him. He drove raises—tunnels straight up—and he never wasted a move.

"Billy Apple's Crew" is true.

Billy Apple's Crew

When you contract in the hardrock mines
You get paid for what you do;
It's my good luck to drill and muck
On Billy Apple's crew, boy
    Billy Apple's crew.

Monday mornin' Bill don't feel good
'Cause he loves the partyin' way;
He leans on a pick and looks real sick
And we don't do much that day, boy
    We don't do much that day.

When Monday's gone we turn it on,
We're a true professional crew;
Bill says, "I feel like drillin' steel!",
'Cause that's what he likes to do, boy
    That's what he likes to do.

Some of the time in the hardrock mine
I'm swingin' a double-jack;
Bill says, "Fine, in six months time
You'll have a new Cadillac, boy!
    Have a new Cadillac!"

First you muck, then timber up,
Then nail the bulkhead down;
You drill and load them eight foot holes
And blast that hardrock down, boy
    Blast that hardrock down.

Now on payday the girls all say
That what they like to do
Is go to town and hang around
With Billy Apple's crew, boy
    Billy Apple's crew.

Hardrock miners drilling underground with stopers or "buzzys"
in the Homestake Gold Mine, Lead, South Dakota
—*Photo courtesy Homestake Mining Company*

The Diesel Band

In 1983 my wife and I sold our cows. The price of cattle was up, we made a little money, and to stave off the tax man I bought a brand new blue-and-white three-quarter-ton Ford diesel pickup. Oh, I loved that truck. Almost as much as my wife did not. You couldn't talk, you see, or listen to the radio. But who cared, as long as you had the sound of that diesel engine in your ears.

I drove that tough truck from my home just out of Three Forks to my job in Butte that whole year listening to the music of its engine.

I'm sure the music in the heart and soul of men and women who drive those eighteen-wheelers responds much the same way to the sound of the music in their Diesel Bands.

The Diesel Band

Signs along the highway are my fans
A Diesel engine is my band
We tune up in the morning and all day long
She makes music, and I sing country songs.

There's rhythm built deep in her soul
Country, bluegrass, rock-and-roll
A touch of throttle—listen to her play
Rollin', rattlin', hammerin' my blues away
Come on Diesel—make some music for me.

We've got songs for sunny days
Or a Rocky Mountain blizzard standing in our way
We carry chains to see us through
And they make music too.

We sing songs about cowboys
We sing about cold steel
We sing of love and loneliness
It depends on the way we feel
And every day we go out and rock-and-roll
On the only broadway we'll ever know
And when I hear the sound that Diesel brings
It makes me want to listen
Lord, it makes me want to sing
Come on Diesel—make some music for me.

There is no highway made too long
No mountain we can't climb
We'll do it with a country song
And she keeps perfect time

And in our favorite truck stop
When the hour is long and late
I take coffee black and strong
And she takes her diesel straight

A Diesel Band makin' music on a Rocky Mountain sunny day

—Photo courtesy Overdrive, The Magazine For The American Trucker

Motor Homin'

When I was young, even when I had a growing family, we did our camping in a tent. I always disdained the sight of those clumsy looking, lumbering boxes on wheels called motorhomes (actually nothing more than a modern adaptation of the prairie schooners that brought our ancestors west.)

Later in life I had the opportunity to own one of these creatures. I was forced to concede that such a mode of travel does cast shadows of doubt on the joys of tent living.

Motor-Homin'

Good mornin', Captain, what do you say?
Well, I've just come rollin' in from back down the way
Fightin' the wind with a tremblin' chin
And two-hundred miles to go yet today.

Where is your prairie, your frontier to roam?
I'll see it from the wheel of my big motor-home
When I pass them little campers, you oughta see 'em scamper
(It's how I get my quota of fun)
I'm a modern-day rover, and I won't move it over
I'm a road-hogging' son-of-a-gun!

Crossin' the prairies is a rough life you find
The freeways are loaded with speed-limit signs
Once I had the feelin' I had to keep a wheelin'
So I let her keep rollin' right through
All the traffic I was passin' till I saw the lights a flashin'
And I learned about the Red and the Blue!

It's mighty rough livin' in this big motor-home
Just beer and beefsteak wherever we roam
With V-8 power, and a good hot shower
And a TV program or two
And if you think we're missin' the kitchen sink, then listen
We even brought that along too!

Jo The Clown

As a young, growing family, we spent some years in Salt Lake City, Utah. While there, for some reason not remembered by any of us, our three older children learned to ride unicycles. One day a stranger saw them plying this new skill, stopped, and invited them to join a clown troupe.

There ensued a couple of unusual seasons of traveling with our kids to various Utah towns and cities, and watching them, as part of this group, dressed and painted artistically as clowns, tie balloon animals, toss candy to kids, and ride unicycles in festive summer parades.

After the work and fun of each parade, there was usually a stop at the nearest fast food joint where the clowning antics reached higher and higher levels of creativity much to the delight not only of the customers, but of the clowns themselves.

One day, following just such a robust session, the leader of the troupe told me the story of Jo The Clown.

Jo The Clown

He was fifty when I met him
    the kind of guy you like
I saw him out there jugglin'
    and ridin' that little bike
He said, "I throw the balls all up
    and then we all fall down,"
And so I came to know
    my new neighbor, Jo, the clown

He said that he'd been clownin'
    for a dozen years or so
Said it made him glad to see
    them kids all laughin' so
Said he really wore a smile
    beneath that painted frown
I was glad I got to know
    my neighbor, Jo, the clown

He got me started clownin'
    he helped me fix my face
Paint and rouge and a rubber nose
    a little out of place
Floppy shoes and baggy pants
    that keep a-fallin' down
We sure do make them kids all laugh
    me and Jo, the clown

One day he said to come and wear
    my brand new clownin' face
We was goin' to do a show
    in a very special place

A hospital for little kids
little kids you see
That hadn't been as lucky
as guys like Jo and me

That's where I met Jo's daughter
as sweet as she could be
Been ridin' in that wheelchair
from the time that she was three
Sometimes it's hard to understand
the way that life comes down
I sure am glad we make 'em laugh
me and Jo, the clown

One Morning At The Sawmill

When he was a very young man he chased very young women; not girls, mind you, very young women. Their perfumes got into him, permeating him from the top of his often fevered brain on down till they mingled with the love tunes frequently expressed through the excited tappings of his toes. The perfumes of different young women were different, but they were all good. With some of the young women he was able to do very well. With others, nothing.

In the spring of the year when he was a very young man, when the snow was gone out of the mountains, he worked with three others cutting timber, getting ready to start a mine by late summer. He got to bed late every night and rose early every morning, and rode to work jammed with the other three into the cab of the small truck, jouncing up the narrow, shaded, water-gullied, rock-studded dirt road.

They liked him he knew, especially the two older, because they teased him about young women, and later he wondered if the perfumes that so permeated him didn't—as he slept on the way to work, the bounce and bob of his head matched to each bounce and bob of the road—effuse from him a soft telltale aroma which filled the truck cab and perhaps provided the two older a pang of sweet regret. They were good to him, and it was good that they were because, when he was a very young man, he was very dumb about most things.

They felled trees and hauled logs, loading the skids at the sawmill, and then they ran the sawmill, transforming the crooked, rough-barked logs into straight, true mine timbers. When the logs were used up they went out and felled more trees and hauled more logs, replenishing the skids. And when the skids were full, they worked in the sawmill again.

The sawmill sat in a soft meadow just beyond a fringe of thick, dark timber, on a sun-washed root of the mountain. In

the spring, the mountain spilled over the sawmill perfumes of blossoms, and berries, and pines, and tender grasses and moist earth, and the thin air itself, apart from those other delicious scents, bore a fragrance all its own. Each time he drew deeply of that sweet soaking perfume it was as the aroma of yet another even more exotic young woman. No matter how deeply he drew it in, no matter how completely it saturated him, he never got enough of it.

Within its perimeter, within its gapped, bark-edged, nailed-up rough-board walls, in addition to those of the mountain, the sawmill preserved smells of its own. The smell of metal, of rail and gear and serrated saw disk, of bearings and grease, of motor and oil and heat, and fuel. They brought fuel each morning, and tipped the can up and as the can glug-slushed its contents into the tank the stink of gas cut across the mountain's perfume like cheap whiskey across the taste of fine wine, and then the gas smell moderated, blended, and became part of the day's perfume.

The sawmill had its own sounds, too. The steady chug of the motor, the song of the bearings, the whisper of the large blade spinning, then shrieking as it chewed into new wood (releasing that lovely aroma). Voices. A laugh. A soft oath. A question. An instruction. The long drive belt, wide as a man's two hands, its ends clenched together in iron teeth hammered down, its frayed surface speeding endlessly, flap, flap, flapping. For Chrissakes, they'd told him, don't get caught in the belt.

There were two ways to start the sawmill motor. One way was for one of the older, Carl usually, because he knew how to do it best, to go around to the front of the motor and jerk the crank until the motor finally started. The other way was easier, for the four to stand in line and pull the belt. It always took two pulls, the first a groan of men and machine, and a belch of gray smoke from the motor's rusted stack, the second a chug, and a chug, and a faster chug, the rhythm speeding up, the

black chuffs of smoke turning gray, then disappearing, leaving only a stem of heat wiggling up out of the pipe. The saw blade whirring. The belt leaping, speeding past.

One morning at the sawmill the motor started on the first pull. He wasn't ready for it. And then a thing happened. And then they went on from there.

Later, each time he returned to the little town and Carl, retired now, was sitting there in his truck, like a small piece of weathered mountain come down there, they talked about present times and past times, but never about the thing that happened. But he carried it with him. And even later when he returned, Carl no longer there, gone like a small important piece of the mountain gone, he carried it with him. The sound of the engine coughing to life on the first pull that morning, the smell of the exhaust spreading down on them, him caught off balance, slowly tipping over onto the speeding belt, and at the end of the belt, waiting, the pulley, and the whirring saw.

The perfumes of the young women and of the mountain and even of the sawmill diminished in him that day, like a fog thinning, and an instinct sharpened, of hard metal and brute mechanical force, of motors, and belts and pulleys, and carelessness, and maimed flesh, and death. He carried it with him, the sight and sound of the belt, him tipping over onto it, and then Carl's arm extending, like rock, steadying him till he straightened and stepped back. Nothing was said. But the belt got no flesh, and the saw got no meat. Not that day. Or ever.

He carried it with him, and at times it came up, reminding him, and it served him well. He never told anyone about it.

But he remembered. And he remembered Carl.

Molly, I'm Older

Much of reality seems to be a figment of the imagination. At an early age we tend to fuel our days on dreams. Sometimes the dreams come true.

As years slip by, the cold truth of our whereabouts can unexpectedly face us, maybe in a mirror on the wall, maybe in a mirror of the mind.

The sudden appearance of that new reality can be a time of bewilderment and despair.

It can be a time of anxiety and loss.

It can be a time of beginning to appreciate what is really important.

Molly, I'm Older

Molly, I'm older, more strands of gray
Pluck 'em right out and just throw 'em away.
When I was a young man I never had time
To look for the good little things you can find
Close to your heart and right there in your mind;
       Molly, I'm older
       I'm older

Molly, I'm lookin', and the face that I see
Lookin' right back now, is that really me?
I don't see the smile and I don't see the dreams
That once were important, and Molly it seems
A short time ago since they were last seen;
       Molly, I'm lookin'
       I'm lookin'

Older and wiser should be the rule
Sometimes the older the bigger the fool
Sometimes I'm ahead, sometimes I'm behind
Sometimes I just take it one step at a time
Sometimes I could laugh
Sometimes I could sing
Let's wait and see, Molly,
What tomorrow will bring

Molly, I'm seein' a tear in your eye
What happened, Molly?
What's makin' you cry?
The way we've been is the way that we'll stay

We've loved each other and life all the way
And you are what matters to me every day;
Molly, I'm seein'
I'm seein'

Tilton home/Robert Vicker home,
Virginia City, Montana — date unknown
—*Photo courtesy The Montana Historical Society, Helena*

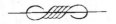

The Hound And The Cat

Once upon a time, in the dog lover's committed world of owning dogs, we bought a purebred Black-and-Tan coonhound.

Now, that dog was a hound in every sense of the word, lean and rangy, large bony bump on the head, a howl that could be heard for at least three miles on a clear summer night, and an intense hatred of all creatures that resemble a raccoon, especially cats.

But not all cats.

The Hound and the Cat

The gray cat steps across the lawn
And the hound dog gives her one big yawn
And drops his head back down, ka-bump,
And gives his tail a single thump.

The cat walks to him, unafraid,
And curls up by him in the shade.
Her feline purr, his canine dreams,
Such peaceful friends it hardly seems

That dog hates every other cat,
And shows them where the real world's at,
And sends them up the nearest tree,
And howls to tear their pedigree.

Now, cats are pretty much the same,
Just different sizes, colors, names,
But the hound dog he don't feel that way,
Can't no other cat beside him lay,

All other cats are his enemies.
It's just that he knows her, don't you see,
Is why he accepts this one gray cat—

Say, aren't us people a lot like that?

He Gathers The Songs

Is one lifetime going to be enough? No. Not the way it looks now. Not for me.

For me, two distinct parts of personality have always existed at the same time in separate places. In the one place, there has been the need to love and cherish wife and family; in the other, there have been such things as all the good ball games needing to be played, all the sleek, fast airplanes needing to be built and flown, and all the writing needing to be written.

For me, the need and duty of the first part has always taken pre-eminence over the second. Yet, that second part has, through an almost spiritual interconnection with grass, trees, wind, and mountain ridges, refused to be ignored.

Day by day the delayed, visceral longings have worked their way out into my songs, where they exist, each one in its own time, each one in its own season.

They, too, are part of the family. They, too, are my children.

He Gathers The Songs

He's lookin' back through all the good things to do
    wonderin' when he grew old
In the day-to-day grind of a life that he finds
    he never brought under control
Makin' ball bearings and motor-bike farings
    eternity ebbin' away
Many's the time he just quit in his mind
    but his body went back the next day.

Sometimes every day stood up in his way
    incredible mountains to climb
At times he could see the best way to be
    was to live it one day at a time
Sometimes he dug deep in the life he was livin'
    lookin' for diamonds and pearls
Sometimes he just wanted to be a folksinger
    more than anything else in the world.

He gathers the songs all around him like children
They each have a name and their own special way
Each one has a time, each one has a season
Each one has a reason for bein' that way
Songs about heartache, songs about love
Songs about Jenny, and he never did know who she was.

In the summertime he's singin' and playin' his guitar
    in the winter he's seein' cloudy days
Sometimes he's bringin' his memories too far
    but mostly he hides them away

He feels like a singer who never learned the notes
playin' melodies he can't recall
Till he starts singin' the songs that he wrote
and that's what he loves most of all.